CEC Mini-Library

**Working with
Behavioral Disorders**

W9-CVV-329

PREPARING TO INTEGRATE STUDENTS WITH BEHAVIORAL DISORDERS

Robert A. Gable, Virginia K. Laycock,
Sharon A. Maroney, and Carl R. Smith

A Product of the ERIC Clearinghouse on Handicapped and Gifted Children
Published by The Council for Exceptional Children

Library of Congress Cataloging-in-Publication Data

Preparing to Integrate students with behavioral disorders / Robert A.
    Gable ... [et al.].
        p.   cm. — (Working with behavioral disorders)
    "CEC mini-library"
    "A product of the ERIC Clearinghouse on handicapped and gifted
children."
    Includes bibliographical references (p.   ).
    ISBN 0-86586-199-4
    1. Handicapped children—Education—United States.
    2. Mainstreaming in education—United States.   I. Gable, Robert A.
    II. Series.
    LC4031.P7   1991
    371.93—dc20   91-3030
                                                                              CIP

ISBN 0-86586-199-4

A product of the ERIC Clearinghouse on Handicapped and Gifted Children

Published in 1991 by The Council for Exceptional Children, 1920 Association
Drive, Reston, Virginia 22091-1589.
Stock No. P340

This publication was prepared with funding from the U.S. Department of
Education, Office of Educational Research and Improvement, contract no.
RI88062007. Contractors undertaking such projects under government sponsor-
ship are encouraged to express freely their judgment in professional and
technical matters. Prior to publication the manuscript was submitted for critical
review and determination of professional competence. This publication has met
such standards. Points of view, however, do not necessarily represent the
official view or opinions of either The Council for Exceptional Children or the
Department of Education.

Printed in the United States of America
10   9   8   7   6   5   4   3   2   1

Contents

Foreword

Working with Behavioral Disorders
CEC Mini-Library

One of the greatest underserved populations in the schools today is students who have severe emotional and behavioral problems. These students present classroom teachers and other school personnel with the challenges of involving them effectively in the learning process and facilitating their social and emotional development.

The editors have coordinated a series of publications that address a number of critical issues facing service providers in planning and implementing more appropriate programs for children and youth with severe emotional and behavioral problems. There are nine booklets in this Mini-Library series, each one designed for a specific purpose.

- *Teaching Students with Behavioral Disorders: Basic Questions and Answers* addresses questions that classroom teachers commonly ask about instructional issues, classroom management, teacher collaboration, and assessment and identification of students with emotional and behavioral disorders.

- *Conduct Disorders and Social Maladjustments: Policies, Politics, and Programming* examines the issues associated with providing services to students who exhibit externalizing or acting-out behaviors in the schools.

- *Behaviorally Disordered? Assessment for Identification and Instruction* discusses systematic screening procedures and the need for functional assessment procedures that will facilitate provision of services to students with emotional and behavioral disorders.

- *Preparing to Integrate Students with Behavioral Disorders* provides guidelines to assist in the integration of students into mainstream settings and the delivery of appropriate instructional services to these students.

- *Teaching Young Children with Behavioral Disorders* highlights the applications of Public Law 99–457 for young children with special needs and delineates a variety of interventions that focus on both young children and their families.

- *Reducing Undesirable Behaviors* provides procedures to reduce undesirable behavior in the schools and lists specific recommendations for using these procedures.

- *Social Skills for Students with Autism* presents information on using a variety of effective strategies for teaching social skills to children and youth with autism.

- *Special Education in Juvenile Corrections* highlights the fact that a large percentage of youth incarcerated in juvenile correctional facilities has special learning, social, and emotional needs. Numerous practical suggestions are delineated for providing meaningful special education services in these settings.

- *Moving On: Transitions for Youth with Behavioral Disorders* presents practical approaches to working with students in vocational settings and provides examples of successful programs and activities.

We believe that this Mini-Library series will be of great benefit to those endeavoring to develop new programs or enhance existing programs for students with emotional and behavioral disorders.

Lyndal M. Bullock
Robert B. Rutherford, Jr.

Preface

This book is divided into two sections. In Part I, Robert A. Gable and Virginia K. Laycock offer some practical advice on how principals, other administrators, and program coordinators can facilitate the integration of students with behavioral disorders into the mainstream of education in an appropriate and orderly way.

Part II, by Sharon A. Maroney and Carl R. Smith, deals with how teachers can better serve students with behavioral disorders by taking responsibility for their own continuing education, collaborative interactions, and the instruction conducted in their classrooms.

Introduction

It is unlikely that educational values and public policy will soon shift from the doctrine of least restrictive environment (LRE). The decision to place a student with exceptionalities in the mainstream is generally predicated on goodness of fit between the demands of the regular classroom setting and the capabilities of the student. Unfortunately, congruence between these two standards is not always feasible (e.g., Kauffman, McCullough, & Saborine, 1984). Accumulated evidence suggests that there are some students who simply cannot be managed and instructed effectively in the regular classroom (e.g., Braaten, Kauffman, Braaten, Polsgrove, & Nelson, 1988).

The more severe the student's behavior problems, the more difficult it usually is to carry out a successful program of instruction in a mainstream setting. Indeed, for some students, greater progress has been documented in special rather than in regular classes (Kauffman & Pullen, 1989). One possible explanation is that the prospect for adoption of proven intervention strategies—especially behavior modification—is greater in special than in general education (e.g., Kauffman & Pullen, 1989). The finite classroom resources of teacher time, skill, and effort make it unlikely that regular class teachers will be able to accommodate many of the population of students with behavioral disorders (BD) (Braaten et al., 1988). For a substantial number of students with BD, the efficacy of the construct of least restrictive environment remains very much in question (Muscott, 1988).

We support the LRE doctrine but take issue with the assumption that students with mild disabilities constitute a homogeneous group whose members can all be viewed in the same way with regard to mainstreaming. It is relevant also that many students with BD who previously were placed in more restrictive out-of-district programs are now back in self-contained or resource classrooms. Accordingly, the composition of the subgroup that once represented the so-called "mildly behaviorally disordered" may well have changed. While the categories of behavioral disorders, mental retardation, and learning disabilities have much in common, maladaptive behavior that includes defiance and aggression is most prevalent among students with BD.

There is ample reason to suggest that we should look critically at educational programming for students with BD apart from other categories of exceptionality. It is imperative that we preserve a range of service options from full integration to separate classrooms and schools that research and experience has shown can benefit students with BD (e.g., Kauffman & Pullen, 1989). We must refine current practices while guarding against any simplistic solutions that may do irreparable harm to students with BD by denying them a full range of service options. It is with these thoughts in mind that we examine aspects of integration and instruction of these students.

Understanding the Resistance to Integration

Students who evidence maladaptive behavior—especially those who engage in bouts of overt aggression—are the ones most often referred for special class placement by regular class teachers. Once a student is classified as behaviorally disordered, he or she is among the least acceptable candidates for integration back into the regular classroom (Braaten et al., 1988; Safran & Lutz, 1984). By most accounts, the negative attitudes that originally aroused regular educators to resist mainstream placement of students with BD have not diminished significantly over the past 10 years (Gable, Hendrickson, Algozzine, & Scully, 1989).

The "disturbingness" perception shared by many general educators is linked to the notion that students with BD are, among other things, inattentive, antisocial, defiant of authority, and disruptive (e.g., Bullock, Zagar, Donahue, & Pelton, 1985). The work of Medway (1979), Safran and Safran (1987), and Gersten, Walker, and Darch (1988) suggests that the attributional assumptions many general educators hold regarding causality and stability of students' behavioral problems, as well as their views on severity, contagion, and manageability of the problems, can contribute to the resistance of these educators to reintegration. Mistaken opinion as to causation of children's behavior disorders has led many general educators to conclude that the problems evidenced by students with BD are beyond the reach of their classroom practices. Finally, fear of the effects of contagion on other students and their own inability to control the situation further reduces the receptivity of regular class teachers to mainstream placement of students with BD.

The probability that teachers will initiate actions to deal with classroom problems is linked to the opinion teachers hold about their ability to manage the situation. Studies show that less than half of the regular class teacher population has received any coursework dealing with specialized instruction (Brown, Gable, Hendrickson, & Algozzine, in press). Other investigations suggest that many regular educators lack the necessary preservice training to deal effectively with learners with exceptionalities (e.g., Baker & Zigmond, 1990; Brown et al., in press). Evidence of the need for specialized instruction is found in the steady decline across grade levels in the provision of individualized instruction for special students and in the fact that general educators do not make use of various strategies that might facilitate the reintegration process (Brown et al., in press).

In light of these facts, it is understandable that few regular educators feel sufficiently prepared to cope with the demands imposed by students with BD and that few special education teachers feel sufficiently prepared to cope with the demands imposed by the integration of BD students into regular classroom programs and into the mainstream of society. It is the purpose of this book to provide both regular educators and special educators with some thoughts on how to provide high-quality education for students with behavioral disorders.

Part I
Organizational and Administrative Aspects of Regular Classroom Integration

Robert A. Gable
Virginia K. Laycock

1. Establishing Guidelines for Integration

Establish clear guidelines to integrate students with behavioral disorders into less restrictive settings in a systematic way.

Only about 50% of all school districts have a written policy governing reintegration. This absence of uniform practices invites inconsistent and arbitrary decision making and seriously impedes the mainstream process (Rizzo & Zabel, 1988). Another problem stems from the fact that too little time is usually allocated to actual reintegration. For example, Laycock and Tonelson (1985) found that 42% of teachers of students with BD who were surveyed reported that the movement of their students from special to regular classrooms was accomplished in only 1 to 4 weeks. These investigators also discovered that there was little attempt to prepare students for a change in placement.

In contrast, regular class integration probably should consist of a multiphase operation that is carried out gradually and systematically and is evaluated at each step. Procedures must be established that have been proven effective and are practical enough for teachers to implement. Muscott and Bond (1986) have offered the following recommendations to facilitate integration of BD students:

- Establish plans to improve the attitude and knowledge of the receiving teacher.
- Provide students with social skills instruction.
- Program for the transfer of training from one setting to another.
- Interface with and coordinate services with mainstream participants.

2. Skills Needed in Regular Classes

Ensure that special education teachers know what skills their students need in order to function effectively in regular classes.

Most teachers of students with behavioral disorders are relatively inexperienced and lack appropriate instruction in the integration process (e.g., Gable et al., 1989; Laycock & Tonelson, 1985; Safran & Safran, 1987). Since few teachers of students with BD are equipped to prepare their students to deal with the rigors of the regular classroom, instruction aimed at "inoculating" students against the vicissitudes of the regular classroom (e.g., fewer curricular modifications, limited use of extrinsic reinforcement) is virtually nonexistent. Only several deliberate attempts to teach students social or school survival skills have been reported in the literature.

For example, Graubard, Rosenberg, and Miller (1974) taught students to make eye contact with teachers, request extra help, and engage in reinforcing behavior such as sitting up straight and nodding in agreement with the teacher. The students were also taught to react to explanations with "Ah-hah." Finally, students were taught to break eye contact when teachers reprimanded them, ignore other teacher provocations, arrive early for class, and request additional assignments. More recently, Morgan, Young, and Goldstein (1983) taught students with BD to prompt teachers to assist them, praise teachers for giving them help, and prompt teachers to show approval of their academic and social performance. These studies are particularly significant because they illustrate ways that practitioners can better prepare students for mainstream placement.

Even when special instruction is initiated, there is another major obstacle related to the fact that few students with BD are able to maintain the skills after instruction is discontinued or generalize them to noninstructional situations. Although much is still unknown, engaging regular class teachers and peers without disabilities in some aspects of reintegration instruction and ongoing support in regular classrooms is one possible solution. Various authors have discussed ways that teachers of students with BD can teach students to engage in norm-referenced, ecologically valid target behaviors; program for their maintenance and generalization; and cast regular classmates in the role of change agent to facilitate that process (e.g., Kerr & Nelson, 1989).

3. Transition Planning

Develop a step-by-step integration process that will help the student make the transition from the practices used in the special classroom to those used in the regular classroom.

Attempts by special educators to apply best practices to the education and treatment of students with behavioral disorders may create a stumbling block to successful regular class placement. As Gable, McConnell, and Nelson (1986) noted, special classroom practices often differ substantially, and they may actually be antithetical to the demands of the regular classroom. For example, programs that rely on complex contingency management plans such as token economies, as well as on strong teacher-pupil interpersonal relationships, may serve to foster student dependency (e.g., Kerr, 1989). Experience has shown that students with BD are sometimes reluctant to leave special programs in favor of less supportive classroom environments.

In recognition of these problems, a step-by-step, graduated instructional process for reintegration is recommended. The content of instruction should probably begin with simple responses that are known to the student, shifting gradually to ecologically valid behavioral demands of less restrictive settings. It may also be important to expose students to some elements of contrasting or "worst practices" that they may encounter after placement in general education (Gable et al., 1986). At first, instruction can be conducted by the special education teacher in the home classroom. Later, other adults should be recruited to carry out instruction in new classroom surroundings, with the ultimate goal being student self-initiation of adaptive behavior. The work of Kerr and Nelson (1983, 1989) contains some excellent suggestions on generalization instruction that include discussion of the role of classmates.

4. Cooperative Planning

Have special class teachers and regular class teachers work together to determine what a student must be able to do, both academically and socially, in order to succeed in the regular classroom.

Few special educators have been taught to identify performance deficits and then assist students with BD to make the necessary adjustments to respond positively to the demands and expectations of the regular classroom (Laycock & Tonelson, 1985). Furthermore, there has been scant research on readiness aspects of reintegration that would give teachers some guidance in preparing students to make a successful transition. Several recent investigations have shed some light on the expectations of regular educators (e.g., Kerr & Zigmond, 1986; Walker & Rankin, 1983). For example, Walker and Rankin concluded that although regular classroom teachers differ significantly, they "hold a narrow, intense, and very demanding" perspective on what behavior is consonant with classroom success (1983). Teacher expectations relate to student compliance, academic productivity, attention to task, and routine-following. Even so, the absence of measurable and objective performance standards at the building and classroom level compels practitioners to rely on subjective opinion to judge whether or not and when to mainstream students.

The inability to assess the ecology of the regular classroom accurately so as to prepare students with BD for it represents another impediment to mainstreaming. The problem is that the special education teacher is powerless to regulate so-called "setting events" (contextual conditions that exist in the regular classroom that do not control behaviors but set the occasion for increasing the likelihood that certain behaviors will occur [Gable, Hendrickson, Warren, Evans, & Evans, 1988]). Setting events have been shown to prompt or inhibit behavior and may contribute to behavioral instability (e.g., when a student is unclear about classroom rules). Classroom conduct, as well as social behavior, is influenced by events that serve as discriminative stimuli (e.g., environmental cues) for students to engage in certain acts (e.g., respond to social bids of classmates; comply with the requests of the teacher).

Some years ago, Grosenick (1971) suggested that teachers should provide students with experiences within special programs that mirror those found in regular classrooms to facilitate generalization of required skills. More recently, Muscott and Bond (1986) and Rizzo and Zabel (1988) recommended the following steps to help facilitate reintegration:

- Ascertain the social and behavioral standards and expectations held by regular classroom teachers.

- Define the treatment goals for each student.

- Establish a means for incorporating into the behavioral repertoire of reintegrated students the social and behavioral concerns of receiving teachers.

Zabel, Peterson, Smith, and White (1982) have shown that a major discrepancy exists between the availability and the usefulness of assessment information at the time decisions are being made about reintegration. The technology required to carry out a thorough assessment of the multiple settings in which students with BD must perform is still in a formative stage. However, some knowledge of setting-specific demands can be gained through direct observation as well as through survey, role play, or interview sources. Few assessment systems have been designed to facilitate this kind of data collection (e.g., instructional environment). Teachers of students with behavioral disorders who are attempting to assess academic readiness for reintegration can also collect work samples from regular class teachers that consist of written products in spelling or arithmetic and audiotapes of student oral reading. Analysis of this material can yield an ecologically valid standard against which to judge the academic performance of students with behavioral disorders (Gable et al., 1986).

5. Enhancing Understanding of Regular Teachers

Expose regular class teachers to students with behavioral disorders in a supportive setting.

There is some evidence that exposure to and experience with students with exceptionalities can moderate the negative views held by some regular class teachers. One way to accomplish this is to engage regular education students in a "reverse mainstreaming" program in which the students (and teachers) spend time in special education classrooms. Another promising practice is "cooperative teaching," in which regular and special educators work in a systematic and coordinated fashion to provide specialized instruction in integrated classrooms (Bauwens, Hourcade, & Friend, 1989). This approach can be especially useful if general educators recognize that best practices in special education have a place and will help improve instruction in the regular classroom. Regardless of the specific strategy, it is important to convey the message that solutions to students' problems *do* exist and that a reasonable amount of effort will usually produce positive changes in pupil behavior. Other valuable advice on helping regular class teachers to overcome their resistance can be found in Margolis and McGettigan (1988) and Friend and Bauwens (1988).

Muscott and Bond (1986), among others, have suggested that receiving teachers should be provided with routine consultation and support on classroom intervention programs for students with BD. However, not all regular educators are receptive to collaboration or the team process of problem solving associated with various support programs such as the Teacher Assistance Team and the School Consultation Committee (see Laycock, Gable, & Korinek, in press). Furthermore, there is some evidence that regular classroom teachers who are most likely to be effective with students with behavior problems often oppose their mainstream placement (Gable et al., 1989). Fortunately, teachers of students with BD can share with regular class teachers knowledge and skills that correspond with instruction not always furnished in other categorical areas (e.g., Wood, 1987). For example, teachers of students with BD usually receive extensive instruction in dealing with conduct and social skills problems; they also are well prepared to adapt the classroom curriculum to accommodate student-specific needs. These are the (e)very areas most often singled out by regular educators who seek assistance in working with students who have special needs.

The success of the reintegration process hinges on the proposition that, given reasonable support, regular educators can successfully instruct students who have a variety of social, academic, and deportment problems (Kerr & Nelson, 1983). However, many regular teachers are not given much assistance in that effort (Gable et al., 1989). One reason is because most teachers of students with BD lack the required preparation to work with their regular class colleagues. We hope that the tremendous surge of interest in preparing regular and special educators to engage in school-based collaboration and consultation will rectify this situation. If high-quality technical assistance can be provided in management and instruction, it is likely that more general educators will accept students with BD in their classrooms.

Conclusion

In concluding the first section, we trust that our attempt to examine some of the variables associated with successful integration has sparked interest in exploring new ways to provide high-quality education for students with behavioral disorders. In the final analysis, we advocate taking a conservative view toward integration and charting the course away from more restrictive placement as carefully as the course toward special education placement (Rizzo & Zabel, 1988). As Kauffman and his colleagues (1984) pointed out, we must strive to establish a consensus that students with behavioral disorders will be reintegrated only when an acceptable match exists between demands of the setting and student capabilities. Only then is it reasonable to envision that regular and special class teachers will be able to work together in support of the reintegration process.

References

Baker, J. M., & Zigmond, N. (1990). Are regular classroom teachers equipped to accommodate students with learning disabilities? *Exceptional Children, 55*, 21–27.

Bauwens, J., Hourcade, J. J., & Friend, M. (1989). Cooperative teaching: A model for general and special education. *Remedial and Special Education, 10*(2), 17–22.

Braaten, S., Kauffman, J. M., Braaten, B., Polsgrove, L., & Nelson, C. M. (1988). The regular education initiative: Patent medicine for behavioral disorders. *Exceptional Children, 55*, 21–27.

Brown, J., Gable, R. A., Hendrickson, J. M., & Algozzine, B. (in press). Prereferral practices of regular teachers: Implications for regular and special teacher preparation. *Teacher Education and Special Education.*

Bullock, L., Zagar, E. L., Donahue, C. A., & Pelton, G. B. (1985). Teachers' perceptions of behaviorally disordered students in a variety of settings. *Exceptional Children, 52*, 123–130.

Friend, M., & Bauwens, J. (1988). Managing resistance: An essential consulting skill for learning disabilities teachers. *Journal of Learning Disabilities, 23*, 556–561.

Gable, R. A., Hendrickson, J. M., Algozzine, B., & Scully, V. (1989). Reintegration of behaviorally disordered students through behavioral consultation. In R. B. Rutherford, Jr., & S. DiGangi (Eds.), *Severe behavior disorders of children and youth* (Vol. 12, pp. 118–131). Reston, VA: Council for Children with Behavioral Disorders.

Gable, R. A., Hendrickson, J. M., Warren, S. F., Evans, W. M., & Evans, S. S. (1988). The promise and pitfalls of an ecological perspective on children's behavior disorders. In R. B. Rutherford, Jr. & J. W. Maag (Eds.), *Severe behavior disorders of children and youth* (Vol. 11, pp. 156–166). Reston, VA: Council for Children with Behavioral Disorders.

Gable, R. A., McConnell, S., & Nelson, C. M. (1986). The learning-to-fail phenomenon as an obstacle to mainstreaming children with behavior disorders. In R. B. Rutherford, Jr., (Ed.), *Severe behavior disorders of children and youth* (Vol. 8, pp. 19–26). Reston, VA: Council for Children with Behavioral Disorders.

Gersten, R., Walker, H., & Darch, C. (1988). Relationship between teachers' effectiveness and their tolerance for handicapped students. *Exceptional Children, 54,* 433–438.

Graubard, P. S., Rosenberg, H., & Miller, M. D. (1974). Student applications of behavior modification to teacher and environments or ecological approaches to social deviancy. In R. Ulrich, T. Stachnik, & J. Mabry (Eds.), *Control of human behavior: Behavior modification in education* (pp. 421–432). Glenview, IL: Scott, Foresman.

Grosenick, J. K. (1971). Integration of exceptional children into regular classrooms: Research and procedures. *Focus on Exceptional Children, 3,* 1–8.

Kauffman, J. M., McCullough, L. L., & Saborine, E. J. (1984). Integrating exceptional students: Problems involving the emotionally disturbed/behaviorally disordered. *B.C. Journal of Special Education, 8,* 201–210.

Kauffman, J. M., & Pullen, P. L. (1989). An historical perspective: A personal perspective on our history of service to mildly handicapped and at-risk students. *Remedial and Special Education, 10*(6), 12–14.

Kerr, M. M. (1989, September). *Why integration fails: The dependency dilemma.* Paper presented at the CEC/CCBD Conference on Behavioral Disorders, Charlotte, North Carolina.

Kerr, M. M., & Nelson, C. M. (1983). *Strategies for managing behavior problems in the classroom.* Columbus, OH: Merrill.

Kerr, M. M., & Nelson, C. M. (1989). *Strategies for managing behavior problems in the classroom* (2nd ed). Columbus, OH: Merrill.

Kerr, M. M., & Zigmond, N. (1986). What do high school teachers want? A study of expectations and standards. *Education and Treatment of Children, 9,* 239–249.

Laycock, V. K., Gable, R. A., & Korinek, L. (in press). Alternative structures for collaboration in the delivery of special services. *Preventing School Failure.*

Laycock, V. K., & Tonelson, S. W. (1985). Preparing emotionally disturbed adolescents for the mainstream: An analysis of current practices. In S. Braatan, R. B. Rutherford, Jr., & W. Evans (Eds.), *Programming for adolescents with behavioral disorders* (Vol. 2, pp. 63–73. Reston, VA: Council for Children with Behavioral Disorders.

Margolis, H., & McGettigan, J. (1988). Managing resistance to instructional modifications in mainstream environments. *Remedial and Special Education, 9*(4), 15–21.

Medway, F. J. (1979). Causal attributes for school-related problems: Teacher perceptions and teacher feedback. *Journal of Educational Psychology, 71,* 809–818.

Morgan, D., Young, K. R., & Goldstein, S. (1983). Teaching behaviorally disordered students to increase teacher attention and praise in mainstreamed classrooms. *Behavioral Disorders, 8,* 265–273.

Muscott, H. S. (1988). The cascade of services model for behaviorally disordered children and youth: Past, present and future perspectives. In R. B. Rutherford, Jr., C. M. Nelson, & S. R. Forness (Eds.), *Bases of severe behavioral disorders in children and youth* (pp. 307–319). Boston: College-Hill.

Muscott, H. S., & Bond, R. (1986). A transitional education model for reintegrating behaviorally disordered students from residential treatment centers to public school programs. In M. K. Zabel (Ed.), *TEACHING: Behaviorally Disordered Youth, 2,* 33–43. Reston, VA: Council for Children with Behavioral Disorders.

Rizzo, J. V., & Zabel, R. H. (1988). *Educating children and adolescents with behavioral disorders: An integrative approach.* Boston: Allyn and Bacon.

Safran, S. J., & Lutz, J. G. (1984). Mainstreaming or mainlining: A competency-based approach to mainstreaming. *Journal of Learning Disabilities, 17,* 27–29.

Safran, S. P., & Safran, J. S. (1987). Perceptions of problem behavior: A review and analysis of research. In R. B. Rutherford, Jr., C. M. Nelson, & S. R. Forness (Eds.), *Bases of severe behavioral disorders in children and youth* (pp. 39–60). Boston: College-Hill.

Walker, H., & Rankin, R. (1983). Assessing the behavior expectations and demands of less restrictive settings. *School Psychology Review, 12,* 274–284.

Wood, F. H. (1987). Issues in the education of behaviorally disordered students. In R. B. Rutherford, Jr., C. M. Nelson, & S. R. Forness (Eds.), *Severe behavior disorders of children and youth* (pp. 15–26). Boston: College-Hill.

Zabel, R. H., Peterson, R. L., Smith, C. R., & White, M. A. (1982). Availability and usefulness of assessment information for emotionally disturbed students. *School Psychology Review, 11*, 433–437.

Part II
Teacher Responsibilities in Providing High-Quality Instruction for Students with Behavioral Disorders

Sharon. A. Maroney
Carl R. Smith

6. Teachers As Advocates

Develop skills in collaboration, advocacy, and designing instructional strategies and program.

Public education is experiencing dramatic change as we enter the 1990s. Roles and responsibilities of most school personnel are being redefined. Today, special education teachers have to be much more adaptable than those of the past. Few teachers enter a system in which they can close the door and "do their own thing," rarely being accountable to others. Whether linked up with their regular education colleagues through the manifestation of the Regular Education Initiative or linked to other agencies' personnel through various mandated interagency arrangements, it is probable that special education teachers do not work alone. Because of this, teachers of students with behavioral disorders need to be capable of not only designing programs and methodologies to provide high-quality education for students and explaining them to others, but also advocating for those programs and methodologies while collaborating and compromising with others. Developing skills in collaboration and advocacy are as essential as developing the skills required to provide high-quality instruction to students with behavioral disorders.

Teachers have to be capable in various collaborative skill areas as they attempt to work as student and program advocates across many different arenas. As Grosenick, George, and George (1987) described it, teachers must be prepared to work much more closely with their colleagues than they did in earlier years.

> Teachers in early classes of the emotionally disturbed did not have broad interactions with the regular educators as their programs were primarily segregated. This contrasts with today's teachers of the behaviorally disordered who, in addition to the responsibilities . . . , are encouraged to involve regular education teachers in the educational process. Teachers of behaviorally disordered students share behavioral interventions, communicate student progress, develop behaviorally disordered students' schedules, and modify the regular education curriculum as evidence of their collaboration with regular education. (p. 165)

Collaborative efforts will mean that teachers of students with behavioral disorders must demonstrate competencies in systems analysis. In addition to the systems analysis role defined for resource teachers, for example (Wiederholt, Hammill, & Brown, 1983), which focuses primarily on the school as a system, teachers of students with BD must be able to analyze and reach out to other systems including families, various community agencies (Mesinger, 1986), social and community groups, legal and correctional agencies, and human service agencies.

It is imperative that teachers of students with BD serve as advocates for these students. At times, these teachers may find themselves loners, without the support of supervisors, principals, or others to whom they are accountable. They have to possess personal criteria for excellence that may or may not be reinforced in the immediate environment. As advocates, they may not always attain the goals they pursue. As Paul (1985) asserted, teachers of students with BD will now be called upon to assert themselves much more strongly than in the past. Such advocates may have to consider the following:

1. Pressure not to identify these children is real and it is not simply based on economic motives. It is rooted in a disturbing political philosophy.

2. We may need more, not less "religious zeal" in advocating the interests of the emotionally disturbed and behaviorally disordered and other handicapped or otherwise vulnerable children and their families.

3. It is at least as much a religious problem as it is scientific. The concern with who is suffering may be a part of a larger question of who will be sacrificed, or who will be able to survive, in an evolutionary process. (Paul, 1985, p. 69)

At a more fundamental level, teachers of students with BD must be concerned with efficient instruction and consistently aware of which are the most relevant skills to be taught. They must be critical consumers of new methodologies and be able to discriminate between methodologies that seem to have empirical validation for the population of students with behavioral disorders and those that may simply be skillfully promoted. As Grosenick and colleagues (1987) asserted, the teacher is the "heart" of the program. Teachers are forced to use wisdom in choosing the most appropriate interventions, and they must have the ability to serve as program designers and evaluators.

The conventional perspective of a teacher of students with BD may be that of someone who carefully designs a program involving intervention strategies such as behavior modification techniques, token economies, reinforcers and punishers, contracts, levels systems, self-management, and possibly time-out procedures—all aimed at changing student behavior. Although this practice is essential in eliminating some behaviors, teachers need to focus more attention on the selection and evaluation of a broader and more generalizable array of instructional strategies. Our use of the term *instructional strategies* will refer to how students are actually taught and the delivery of instruction throughout all areas of the educational program.

In one attempt to define high-quality instructional programs, a components approach to instruction for students with BD was recently developed in Iowa (Sodac, McGinnis, Smith, Wood, Dystra, & Brees, 1988). This example defines a comprehensive program for such students through the inclusion of the following components:

I. A description of the means by which desirable behaviors will be rewarded and increased.

II. A description of the means by which undesirable behaviors will be dealt with and decreased, including crisis management techniques and planned disciplinary procedures, if necessary.

III. Goals and objectives reflecting interventions to improve interpersonal relationship skills or personal adjustment of the pupil, which may include social skills training, affective or emotional growth strategies, and/or self-control strategies.

IV. Goals and objectives reflecting alternative academic instructions and/or functional skill development based on special education needs of pupils.

V. A reintegration plan specifying how the above areas will be taught in such a way as to provide for generalization and maintenance of newly learned skills in settings outside of the training situation. (p. 7)

It is believed that components III, IV, and V reflect the greatest instructional challenges for the field of behavioral disorders today. (Readers are referred to the following sources for extended information on components I and II: Davis & Brower, 1988; Marshall & Woodard, 1988; Snell, 1987).

When selecting instructional strategies that meet these instructional challenges, teachers should consider the following six criteria. They should be

- Efficient, effective, and empirically demonstrated.
- Adaptable and capable of promoting generalization and maintenance.
- Communicated and understood.
- Responsive to the current needs of the constituent society.
- Receptive and reflective of technology.
- Responsive to student academic, cognitive, social, and affective needs.

These six criteria will be reflected in points 7 through 14 in the following sections.

7. Evaluating Student Progress

Learn how to evaluate student progress in order to deliver instruction most efficiently and effectively.

With the continually growing demands being placed on teachers and the constantly expanding amount of information students are being required to learn, it is necessary to use the most efficient instructional strategies. An efficient instructional strategy can be defined as one that produces the greatest amount of gain while requiring the smallest amount of resources. Strategies selected must be those that make the least demand on teacher preparation, presentation, and follow-up time and efforts, as well as materials and monetary costs, while resulting in high levels of student learning.

Instructional strategies must be effective in producing the desired outcome. This may seem obvious, but there are teachers who select their methods of instruction at the beginning of the year and continue to employ them without systematic efforts to document effectiveness (Bender & Ikechukwa, 1989). Except in empirical studies, the effectiveness of instructional strategies is rarely evaluated and compared in classroom settings. In few, if any, other professions is it acceptable to select and continue to use a method without evaluating its effectiveness against functional standards or alternative methods.

Special educators must be skilled at implementing techniques such as "diagnostic teaching" or "diagnostic probes" (McLoughlin & Lewis, 1986) to evaluate the effectiveness of alternative instructional strategies with students with behavioral disorders (Gable, Hendrickson, & Mercer, 1985). *Diagnostic teaching* is a systematic method of evaluating the effectiveness of two or more instructional techniques, whereas *diagnostic probes* are used to evaluate the effect of changing some aspect of a classroom task on student performance (McLoughlin & Lewis, 1986).

Once selected, instructional strategies must lend themselves readily to the frequent, accurate, and efficient collection of data on student progress. That information must be collected routinely, not only in assessing the accomplishment of individualized education program (IEP) goals, but also in evaluating and planning instructional strategies used in the classroom (Fuchs, Fuchs, & Hamlett, 1989; McLoughlin & Lewis, 1986). Teachers of students with BD must be data-responsible and able to make timely and appropriate programming decisions.

Reisberg and Wolf's (1988) application of the principle of parsimony emphasizes the necessity of efficiency and effectiveness in selecting instructional strategies. They proposed that when more than one strategy might work selection should be based on the simpler and more direct approach to arrive at the desired instructional goal. This criterion cannot be met solely through subjective impressions of a particular strategy; it must involve ongoing collection of classroom data on student progress.

The instructional strategies applied to teaching students with BD must also have a certain degree of empirical support; they must be field-validated and proven effective. Although it is unrealistic to expect that an instructional strategy will be studied in all environments, with all types of students and teachers, and over an extended time period, teachers must select strategies that are supported by a reasonable degree of sound research effort.

8. Generalizing Skills

Teach students skills that are useful in a variety of settings and can be generalized and maintained.

The need to increase the degree of generalization and maintenance of the skills and information taught to students in special education programs has arisen primarily from two sources: the pressure to increase accountability (Reynolds & Wang, 1983) and the increased mainstreaming and cross-environmental programming of students with disabilities. Therefore, instructional strategies must be adaptable across settings, across educators, across students, and across circumstances.

Although the idea is not universally supported, the probable direction for programs for students with behavioral disorders in the future is that more students will be served in regular classroom settings (Reynolds, Wang, & Walberg, 1987), while those with severe disorders will be served in a combination of regular classroom, self-contained, and alternative settings (Morgan & Jenson, 1988). Strategies chosen to instruct these students must be effective in differing environments and adaptable to the needs of special education and regular education teachers as well as to those of persons in the natural environment who will assist in programming (e.g., agency workers, parents).

A second probable direction, directly related to the placement of students in regular education classes, is the increased use of group instruction and the decreased use of one-on-one instruction. This will result in an increased use of instructional programs involving social skills, cooperative learning, and peer-oriented instruction. Reisberg and Wolf (1988) recognized the need to select group instructional strategies with respect to adaptability across members in the group. They proposed following the "principle of generalized benefit," which suggests selecting strategies that can benefit more than one student at a time. This concept ties into the need to select instructional strategies that are adaptable as well as efficient in group instruction.

Instructional strategies must be adaptable for both teachers and students. Teachers must select strategies that they can easily adapt to meet the purpose of instruction, the content, the instructional medium, the needs of students, the setting, and the concept of the "teachable moment." Strategies such as computer-assisted instruction or programs such as DISTAR (Engelmann & Bruner, 1975) may be limited in their adaptability because of their requirements for equipment or structure, whereas peer learning activities (Hawryluk & Smallwood, 1988) or self-control techniques (Meyen, Vergason, & Whelan, 1988) may be more easily adaptable for both teachers and students.

Students must also be instructed through the use of strategies that they can adapt and use as they learn other skills in other settings. The current demands of society, which require that individuals be independent learners who assume responsibility for their own learning and are able to adapt to the changes in those societal demands, are likely to increase over the next 10 years. Students must be adept at acquiring new information and developing new methods of responding. Instructional strategies that promote student initiative in learning such as the learning strategy approach, self-management, problem solving, and thinking skills (Delagardelle & Studer, 1988) are methods of responding to this demand. Conversely, strategies that are primarily teacher led and teacher controlled limit students' ability to independently adopt and adapt those strategies to other learning situations. The instructional strategies selected by teachers must promote independent and responsible learners who can use those strategies in various ways.

While a modest body of research has suggested that students with behavioral disorders can demonstrate learning in the instructional setting and under the direction of the individual guiding that instruction, the degree to which that learning is generalized and maintained in other settings is often inadequate (Morgan & Jenson, 1988; Snell, 1987). *Generalization* is said to have taken place when behavior learned in one situation occurs in another situation (Holvik & Benskin, 1988), whereas *maintenance* pertains to skills and behaviors that persist over time, are durable, and are resistant to extinction (Holvik & Benskin, 1988). The current need is to identify and use instructional strategies that facilitate the generalization and maintenance of learning to functional criterion levels for the students. Instructional activities that fail to produce generalization and maintenance of student learning must be questioned in light of the demand for educational accountability, responsibility, and professionalism.

9. Communicating Clearly

Use language that is clear and free of jargon in all communications about programs, strategies, and students.

We only need to open a textbook, a journal, or the recently published *Dictionary of Special Education and Rehabilitation* (Vergason, 1990) to be aware of the widespread use of professional jargon and the emergence of new terms and definitions in the field of special education. Although the growth of new and unique vocabulary and acronyms may serve some worthwhile purposes, this practice significantly decreases the ease with which communication and understanding are shared between educators and parents, as well as between professional disciplines and various larger sections of society. Literature on the involvement and reaction of parents of students in special education underscores the effect of the use of professional jargon in creating parental discomfort (Turnbull & Turnbull, 1986) and decreasing parents' willingness to participate in special education activities. Overreliance on technical and scientific terminology is also one possible impediment to communication of research information to practitioners (Shaver, 1982).

Recognizing the barriers that are sometimes erected with terminology, educators must work toward the effective, accurate, and efficient communication of the strategies they select. The vocabulary used should be easily understood, as well as consistent across disciplines, and should aim toward generality rather than specificity. The cooperative teaching model presented by Bauwens, Houracde, and Friend (1989) necessitates such communication of instructional strategies between regular and special educators. In this model, as in many interdisciplinary efforts, a lack of communication and understanding significantly limits the ability to teach and work cooperatively.

The current increased emphasis on interagency collaboration and the involvement of the community in educational programs for students with BD increases the need for communication and understanding across disciplines and throughout society. The use of technical and scientifically derived vocabulary, although it may reflect improvements in the research methodology of special education, has limited practicality in efforts to increase interagency communication. Accurate, effective, and efficient communication and understanding should not be limited to the definitions of instructional strategies; they should also include the procedures connected with those strategies.

10. From Classroom to Real Life

Prepare students for the realities of contemporary life beyond the classroom.

Instructional strategies selected by teachers must be responsive to the current needs and values of society and to changes in those needs and values. The needs and values of society differ with respect to variables such as locale, time period, political agendas, current events, economics, employment, and culture. Currently, educational programs should be responding to societal concerns such as the war on drugs, the homeless, the rights of parents and children, AIDS, and the dropout population. Programs in the future may need to respond to continuations or variations of these issues in addition to a yet unknown set of societal concerns.

A sensitivity to the current needs of society is not meant to imply that these programs should merely be agents of society charged with the responsibility for shaping students according to societal wishes. Rather, it is meant to imply that programs should be guided by and based on the realities of the societal expectations that will be faced by the students served.

In 1978, Wolf proposed the adoption of the concepts of social validation and social importance in the design, implementation, and evaluation of behavior change programs. He proposed methods of determining the degree of importance a sample of the population held for various behavior, changes in behavior, procedures used, and the evaluation of the outcomes of behavior change programs. As noted by Cullinan, Epstein, and Reimers (1981), while until now the greatest degree of application of these concepts has been within the field of mental retardation, the field of behavioral disorders is beginning to recognize and apply the concepts of social validation and social importance. Although these applications have typically been made in conjunction with social skills instruction programs, it appears equally important that they be incorporated into the selection of instructional strategies.

11. Strategies That Work

Use instructional strategies that are known to work.

Teacher effectiveness research suggests that teacher skills in organizing and managing classroom activities and presenting instructional material, in addition to the development of positive teacher-student relationships, are the most important factors influencing student behavior (Jones & Jones, 1990). Kounin (1970), Brophy and Good (1986), and Emmer, Evertson, Sanford, Clements, and Worsham (1982) have identified a set of specific teacher behaviors that facilitate learning and prevent disruption during instructional activities. *Direct instruction,* a strategy that involves a specific lesson structure and a procedure for carrying out the lesson, incorporates many of these teacher behaviors in efforts to maximize student learning and minimize off-task behavior (Fernandez & Kodros, 1988). In direct instruction, the use of strategies such as group instruction, teacher-directed learning, frequent responses, and structured student practice have been shown to have a positive influence on student achievement.

Weade and Evertson (1988) studied the effect of differing instructional lessons with respect to the changes in social and academic task demands required of the students during any one lesson. An illustration of a change in a social task demand would be the change from asking students to answer questions orally to asking them to work with a peer in completing a written task. Examples of academic task demands include reading, writing, filling in the blanks, and generating original sentences. Weade and Evertson (1988) found that more effective teachers, as determined by measures of student achievement, employed fewer changes in task demands and sustained the instructional focus for longer periods of time. Although some caution is required in generalizing across populations of students, this finding seems particularly noteworthy when working with students with BD—students who typically do not adjust well to change.

Taking a closer view of the use of instructional time in the classroom has been the subject of a number of investigations (Berliner, 1988; Ysseldyke, Thurlow, Christenson, & Weiss, 1987; Ysseldyke, Thurlow, Mecklenberg, & Graden, 1984). The importance of these studies lies in the fact that increases in active student engagement time have been shown to lead to increases in achievement (Mastropieri & Scruggs, 1987). Some studies have found that only 44% of the time allocated for instruction is spent in active engagement by students (Mastropieri & Scruggs, 1987). The consensus appears to be that it is important not only to maximize the total amount of time allocated for instruction but also to study how much of that time is spent by students actively engaged in academic attending, responding, and practice.

12. Teaching Responsibility to Students

Teach students the skills needed to take responsibility for their own learning.

Woven within a number of the stated criteria for instruction of students with behavioral disorders is the need to increase student independence in learning. Students with BD may be particularly uninvolved in their learning due to problems with self-concept, lack of a feeling of belonging to the school, and their experiences with repeated failures in school. Instructional strategies involving self-control, self-reinforcement, self-monitoring, self-management, problem solving, cognitive behavior modification, and metacognitive skills (Delagardelle & Studer, 1988; Deshler & Schumaker, 1988; Marshall & Woodard, 1988; Meyen et al., 1988) focus primarily on teaching students the skills necessary for taking responsibility and showing initiative in making decisions regarding their own instruction. These strategies, typically used in combination or in a "package format" that incorporates extrinsic reinforcement, have shown promise for enhancing student learning and independence (Hughes, Ruhl, & Misra, 1989). Although these programs may require considerable teacher preparation time in the initial stages of implementation, this is more than compensated for by the increases in students' independence and responsibility for their own learning.

Acts of aggression are a major stumbling block for many students with behavioral disorders. An interesting and promising program recently developed by Goldstein and Glick (1987), Aggression Replacement Training, coordinates the strategies of structured learning and anger control instruction with moral education. "Moral reasoning has been included in the hope that once a youngster has been provided with prosocial and self-control skills, he will then choose to use these skills in a self-enhancing manner . . . ." (Delagardelle & Studer, 1988, p. 163).

The Strategies Intervention Model (SIMS) (Deshler & Schumaker, 1988) is a program specifically designed to teach students with mild disabilities and those who are low achievers to become independent learners. As described by Deshler and Schumaker (1988),

> the primary emphasis is on teaching students how to learn and how to perform academic, social, or job-related tasks in order to cope with immediate demands as well as to generalize these skills to similar tasks in different settings under different conditions throughout their lives. (p. 393)

This program was also designed to reflect the fact that students are taught in and learn in multiple settings, that cooperation among teachers must increase, that generalization and maintenance must be planned for if it is to occur, and that involvement of individuals outside the classroom is needed (Deshler & Schumaker, 1988). The SIMS program incorporates the Learning Strategies Curriculum as developed by Deshler and his colleagues, a primary component in teaching students skills for independent learning. This curriculum is organized into three strands of student skills: strategies that help students acquire information from written materials, strategies that enable students to identify and store information, and strategies that facilitate written expression and student ability to demonstrate competence (Deshler & Schumaker, 1988).

In providing high-quality instruction for students with behavioral disorders, teachers must select strategies that will facilitate student independence in learning. To function adequately in our society, students must be able to take control of their own life-long learning in order to meet the changing demands in the environment.

13. Teaching Social Skills

Make social skills instruction a significant part of the curriculum.

Instruction to increase social functioning and social competence of students—social skills instruction (Green-Sommerville & Nichols, 1988; Gresham, 1981; Knoff, 1988)—will continue to be a necessary component in programs for students with behavioral disorders. However, there is scant evidence that instruction in social skills has led to improved peer interactions in natural settings. Emphasis must be directed toward increasing the generalization and maintenance of the skills taught, employing socially valid information in the selection of skills to teach and the evaluation of outcomes, and building the social competence of students.

> [G]eneralization rarely occurs unless it has been carefully and purposefully programmed . . . . [T]here are very few shortcuts to achieving generalized changes in behavior. It is very likely that ensuring generalization will require at least as much thought and effort (and probably more) as was required to obtain improvements in the treatment setting. (Morgan & Jenson, 1988, pp. 154, 157)

As others have long asserted, educators must stop using the "train-and-hope" approach (Stokes & Baer, 1977) and must incorporate instructional techniques that will facilitate the generalization and maintenance of social skills learned as an integral part of their instructional program. Strategies to promote generalization and maintenance need to be discussed and selected in the preplanning phase of any instruction (Snell, 1987). In their text *Teaching Behaviorally Disordered Students: Preferred Practices,* Morgan and Jenson (1988) presented a number of instructional strategies that can facilitate the generalization and maintenance of skills learned. A second source is Snell's (1987) text *Systematic Instruction of Persons with Severe Handicaps,* Third Edition. Although this text is primarily directed at the instruction of students with severe and multiple disabilities, the techniques presented are particularly applicable to students with behavior disorders because of their focus on systematic instruction, behavioral principles, and promotion of the criterion of ultimate functioning (Brown, Nietupski, & Hamre-Nietupski, 1976).

A recent study by Maroney (1989) offers a new application for the use of socially valid information in developing instructional programs to increase the social functioning of students with BD. In this investigation, information was collected from high school students with respect to the importance of a set of social skills. The results indicated that, while all groups consistently identified a subset of the most important and the least important skills, there were significant differences in the ratings of individual skills with respect to the students' sex, age, and type of community of residence. Informal discussions have indicated that special education professionals are not able to predict what information was collected from this sample of high school students. This work supports the potential value of gathering group-specific socially valid information to identify social skills objectives. Then the actual worth of the targeted skills can be evaluated.

Many students with BD have particular difficulties with and lack skill in the area of social competence. The term *social competence* refers here to students' ability to use environmental cues and alter their social behavior in eliciting the desired consequences that follow that behavior. If our goal is to improve the overall functioning of these students, social skills instruction must play a major role. A major challenge, however, is that social competence poses significant problems because of the complexities and demands of varying social situations, human beings, and the skills required in the perception and interpretation of social events. Continued research efforts need to be directed toward ways to improve our ability to teach enough of the required skills to improve students' social competence.

A second area of instruction that can serve to increase social functioning of students with behavioral disorders involves instruction within the affective domain. (Eberle & Hall, 1975; Fairchild, 1988; Grosenick, Huntze, McGinnis, & Smith, 1984).

> Broadly stated, the affective domain may be described as the realm of feelings, an understanding of which leads to the development of attitudes, values, and emotional control. One's self-esteem, one's attitude towards others, one's capacity for warm interpersonal relationships are concerns of the affective domain. (Moyer in Eberle & Hall, 1975, p. ii)

The future will not only require students to be responsible for continuing their own learning, but also offer many more choices for individuals. Affective education holds promise as a tool to increase the individual's ability to set priorities and make better choices.

The instructional strategies used in cooperative learning activities (Johnson & Johnson, 1975) and activities that involve peers as instructional agents (Hawryluk & Smallwood, 1988) are a third area that holds promise for increasing social functioning of students. Programs such as peer-assisted learning (PAL) combine peer tutoring and cooperative group learning techniques to engage students in structured interactions to accomplish a specific task. They have been shown to increase some student achievement as well as social and emotional growth (Hawryluk & Smallwood, 1988). Because of the beneficial effects of the tutoring experience on tutors themselves (e.g., academic gains through organizing instruction and acting as a tutor; positive effects on the student tutor's self-image), having students with behavioral disorders serve as peer tutors or group leaders seems to be a worthwhile application of this form of instruction.

14. Improving Quality of Life

Provide students with a functional curriculum that will provide skills and information that will directly serve to improve their ultimate quality of life.

The adoption of a functional curriculum is a common practice in serving students with more serious mental retardation and multiple disabilities. The focus is on teaching skills that can directly improve the ultimate functioning of the student and the quality of his or her life (Brown et al., 1976; Snell, 1987). Although the skills selected will differ, the adoption of a functional curriculum approach should also be applied to students with BD. The concept of functional skills is not limited to the areas of self-help or community mobility, but can also include skills such as those required to seek and access assistance, be life-long independent learners, respond to changes in the environment, succeed in employment, be adequately functioning adults and parents, and achieve satisfying and productive lives. The concepts of the functional curriculum approach, the criterion of ultimate functioning, and participation to the highest degree possible in life must be extended to students with BD, many of whom will otherwise fail to fulfill their potential.

A second area that must be addressed in order to enable access to and functioning in society is the incorporation of state-of-the-art technology in instructional programs. Like others in society, students with behavioral disorders must be experienced with, comfortable with, and able to use a wide variety of technological media. This need is sure to increase in the future.

Although teachers' current use of computer-based instruction may be somewhat limited, and "far from the cutting edge" (Okolo, Rieth, & Bahr, 1989, p. 108), the whole field of computer-based instruction and technology-oriented instruction holds tremendous promise (Kulik & Kulik, 1987). The use of computer-based instruction has been linked to increased motivation for learning tasks (Malouf, 1988); improved achievement; generalized increased achievement on related seatwork

(Malouf, 1988); improved self-efficacy ratings of competency on academic tasks (Graham & MacArthur, 1988); and increased active engagement during computer instruction (Graham & MacArthur, 1988). The work of Hasslebring (1989) holds still further promise with respect to increasing the automaticity of student performance on computers and developing programs that incorporate multiple technological media in present instruction.

Teachers who fail to be knowledgeable about and skillful in employing technological advancements are limiting the ability of their students to function in today's environment.

Conclusion

Within the area of behavioral disorders, the need to promote, accept, and value individuality across students and groups has often been promoted. The popular phrase "Celebrate Deviance" needs to be extended to the true celebration of differences. As stated by Semmel (1987),

> Special educational curricula and interventions must be seen in the context of a broader societal response to individual differences. However, interventions should not seek to eliminate those valued individual and group differences that serve to define the diversity of our democratic society so admirably. (p. 321)

We acknowledge that many students with BD exhibit differences that are seriously aberrant and unacceptable. In such cases, there is little question regarding the need to develop more conforming behaviors to increase functioning in society. But caution needs to be taken when educational practices require the student to meet the needs of the program, the classroom, the instructional activity, the curriculum content, or the method of evaluation. The role of conformity in the classroom should be evaluated. The focus of both education and society must be toward establishment of a "goodness of fit" between the person and society along with an appreciation of differences.

References

Bauwens, J., Hourcade, J. J., & Friend, M. (1989). Cooperative teaching: A model for general and special education integration. *RASE, 10*(2), 17–22.

Bender, W. N., & Ikechukwa, C. U. (1989). Instructional strategies in mainstream classrooms: Prediction of the strategies teachers select. *RASE, 10*(2), 23–30.

Berliner, D. (1988). Effective classroom management and instruction: A knowledge base for consultation. In J. L. Graden, J. E. Zins, & M. J. Curtis (Eds.), *Alternative educational delivery systems: Enhancing instructional options for all students* (pp. 309–326). Washington, DC: National Association of School Psychologists.

Brophy, J., & Good, T. L. (1986). Teacher behavior and student achievement. In M. C. Witirock (Ed.), *Handbook of research on teaching* (3rd ed.). New York: Macmillan.

Brown, L., Nietupski, J., & Hamre-Nietupski, S. (1976). Criterion of ultimate functioning. In M. A. Thomas (Ed.), *Hey don't forget about me* (pp. 2–15). Reston, VA: The Council for Exceptional Children.

Cullinan, D., Epstein, M. H., & Reimers, C. (1981). Social validation: Evaluating the effectiveness of interventions with behaviorally disordered pupils. In F. H. Wood (Ed.), *Perspectives for a New Decade* (pp. 63–71). Reston, VA: The Council for Exceptional Children.

Davis, M., & Brower, D. (1988). Increasing desirable behaviors. In D. Sodac, E. McGinnis, C. Smith, F. Wood, D. Dykstra, & N. Brees (Eds.), *The Iowa program standards for interventions in behavioral disorders* (pp. 53–64). Des Moines: Iowa Department of Education.

Delagardelle, M., & Studer, M. (1988). Self-control strategies. In D. Sodac, E. McGinnis, C. Smith, F. Wood, D. Dykstra, & N. Brees (Eds.), *The Iowa program standards for interventions in behavioral disorders* (pp. 149–170). Des Moines: Iowa Department of Education.

Deshler, D. D., & Schumaker, J. B. (1988). An instructional model for teaching students how to learn. In J. L. Graden, J. E. Zins, & M. J. Curtis (Eds.), *Alternative educational delivery systems: Enhancing instructional options for all students* (pp. 391–412). Washington, DC: National Association of School Psychologists.

Eberle, B., & Hall, R. E. (1975). *Affective education guidebook: Classroom activities in the realm of feelings.* Buffalo, NY: D.O.K. Publishers.

Emmer, E. T., Evertson, C. M., Sanford, J. P., Clements, B. S., & Worsham, M. E. (1984). *Classroom management for secondary teachers.* Englewood Cliffs, NJ: Prentice-Hall.

Engelmann, S., & Bruner, E. (1975). *DISTAR reading.* Chicago: Science Research Associates.

Fairchild, D. (1988). Affective/emotional growth. In D. Sodac, E. McGinnis, C. Smith, F. Wood, D. Dykstra, & N. Brees (Eds.), *The Iowa program standards for interventions in behavioral disorders* (pp. 131–148). Des Moines: Iowa Department of Education.

Fernandez, L., & Kodros, N. (1988). Functional skill development. In D. Sodac, E. McGinnis, C. Smith, F. Wood, D. Dykstra, & N. Brees (Eds.), *The Iowa program standards for interventions in behavioral disorders* (pp. 173–204). Des Moines: Iowa Department of Education.

Fuchs, L. S., Fuchs, D., & Hamlett, C. L. (1989). Effects of instrumental use of curriculum-based measurement to enhance instructional programs. *RASE, 10*(2), 43–52.

Gable, R. A., Hendrickson, J. M., & Mercer, C. O. (1985). A classroom-based curriculum validation process for teaching the behavior disordered. In M. K. Zabel (Ed.), *TEACHING: Behavior disordered youth* (pp. 1–11). Reston, VA: Council for Children with Behavioral Disorders.

Goldstein, A. P., & Glick, B. (1987). *Aggression replacement training: A comprehensive intervention for aggressive youth.* Champaign, IL: Research Press.

Graham, S., & MacArthur, C. (1988). Improving learning disabled students' skills at revising essays produced on a word processor: Self-instructional strategy training. *Journal of Special Education, 22*(2), 133–152.

Green-Somerville, M., & Nichols, P. (1988). Social skills training. In D. Sodac, E. McGinnis, C. Smith, F. Wood, D. Dykstra, & N. Brees (Eds.), *The Iowa program standards for interventions in behavioral disorders* (pp. 103–127). Des Moines: Iowa Department of Education.

Gresham, F. (1981). Social skills training with handicapped children: A review. *Review of Educational Research, 51*(1), 139–176.

Grosenick, J. K., George, M. P., & George, N. L. (1987). A profile of school programs for the behaviorally disordered: Twenty years after Morse, Cutler, and Fink. *Behavioral Disorders, 12*(3), 159–168.

Grosenick, J. K., Huntze, S. L., McGinnis, E., & Smith, C. R. (Eds.). (1984). *Social/affective interventions in behavioral disorders.* Des Moines: Iowa Department of Education.

Hasselbring, T. (1989, October). *Using computers with students having mild mental retardation.* Paper presented at the Council for Exceptional Children's Second International Conference on Mental Retardation: Best Practices in Mental Retardation. Davenport, Iowa.

Hawryluk, M. K., & Smallwood, D. L. (1988). Using peers as instructional agents: Peer tutoring and cooperative learning. In J. L. Graden, J. E. Zins, & M. J. Curtis (Eds.), *Alternative educational delivery systems: Enhancing instructional options for all students* (pp. 371–390). Washington, DC: National Association of School Psychologists.

Holvik, L., & Benskin, J. (1988). Generalization and maintenance. In D. Sodac, E. McGinnis, C. Smith, F. Wood, D. Dykstra, & N. Brees (Eds.), *The Iowa program standards for interventions in behavioral disorders* (pp. 257–272). Des Moines: Iowa Department of Education.

Hughes, C. A., Ruhl, K. L., & Misra, A. (1989). Self-management with behaviorally disordered students in school settings: A promise unfulfilled? *Behavioral Disorders, 14*(4), 250–262.

Johnson, D. W., & Johnson, R. T. (1975). *Learning together and alone: Cooperation, competition, and individualization.* Englewood Cliffs, NJ: Prentice-Hall.

Jones, V. F., & Jones, L. S. (1990). *Comprehensive classroom management: Motivating and managing students* (3rd ed.). Boston: Allyn and Bacon.

Knoff, H. M. (1988). Effective social interventions. In J. L. Graden, J. E. Zins, & M. J. Curtis (Eds.), *Alternative educational delivery systems: Enhancing instructional options for all students* (pp. 431–453). Washington, DC: National Association of School Psychologists.

Kounin, J. (1970). *Discipline and group management in classrooms.* New York: Holt, Rinehart, and Winston.

Kulik, J. A., & Kulik, C. C. (1987). Review of recent research literature on computer-based instruction. *Contemporary Educational Psychology, 12*, 222–230.

Malouf, D. B. (1988). The effects of instructional computer games on continuing student motivation. *Journal of Special Education, 21*(4), 27–38.

Maroney, S. A. (1989). A social validation study of Iowa high school students' ratings of importance of selected individual social skills with respect to peer acceptance. (Doctoral dissertation, University of Minnesota, 1989). *Dissertation Abstracts International, 50*, 2861–3027.

Marshall, A., & Woodard, B. (1988). Managing and decreasing undesirable behaviors. In D. Sodac, E. McGinnis, C. Smith, F. Wood, D. Dykstra, & N. Brees (Eds.), *The Iowa program standards for interventions in behavioral disorders* (pp. 65–100). Des Moines: Iowa Department of Education.

Mastropieri, M. A., & Scruggs, T. E. (1987). *Effective instruction for special education.* Boston: College-Hill.

McLoughlin, J. A., & Lewis, R. B. (1986). *Assessing special students* (2nd ed.). Columbus, OH: Merrill.

Mesinger, J. F. (1986). Alternative education for behaviorally disordered youth: A promise yet unfulfilled. *Behavioral Disorders, 11*(2), 98–108.

Meyen, E. L., Vergason, G. A., & Whelan, R. J. (1988). *Effective instructional strategies for exceptional children.* Denver: Love.

Morgan, D. P., & Jenson, W. R. (1988). *Teaching behaviorally disordered students.* Columbus, OH: Merrill.

Okolo, C. M., Rieth, H. J., & Bahr, C. M. (1989). Microcomputer implementation of secondary special education programs: A study of special educators,' mildly handicapped adolescents,' and administrators' perspectives. *Journal of Special Education, 23*(1), 107–117.

Paul, J. L. (1985). Behavioral disorders in the 1980's: Ethical and ideological issues. *Behavioral Disorders, 11* (1), 66–72.

Reisberg, L., & Wolf, R. (1988). Instructional strategies for special education consultants. *RASE, 9*(6), 29–40.

Reynolds, M. C., & Wang, M. C. (1983). Restructuring "special" school programs: A position paper. *Policy Studies Review, 2*(1), 189–212.

Reynolds, M. C., Wang, M. C., & Walberg, H. J. (1987). The necessary restructuring of regular and special education. *Exceptional Children, 53*, 391–398.

Semmel, M. I. (1987). Special education in the year 2000 and beyond: A proposed action agenda for addressing selected ideas. In H. J. Prehm (Ed.), *The future of special education* (pp. 4–21). Reston, VA: The Council for Exceptional Children.

Shaver, J. P. (1982). *Making research useful for teachers*. Paper presented at the annual meeting of the National Council for the Social Studies, Boston, Massachusetts. (ERIC Document Reproduction Service No. ED 224 754.)

Snell, M. E. (1987). *Systematic instruction of persons with severe handicaps* (3rd ed.). Columbus, OH: Merrill.

Sodac, D., McGinnis, E., Smith, C., Wood, F., Dykstra, D., & Brees, N. (Eds.). (1988) *The Iowa program standards in behavioral disorders*. Des Moines: Iowa Department of Education.

Stokes, T. F., & Baer, D. M. (1977). An implicit technology of generalization. *Journal of Applied Behavioral Analysis, 10*, 349–367.

Turnbull, A. P., & Turnbull, H. R. (1986). *Families, professionals, and exceptionality: A special partnership*. Columbus, OH: Merrill.

Vergason, G. A. (1990). *Dictionary of special education and rehabilitation* (3rd ed.). Denver: Love.

Weade, R., & Evertson, C. M. (1988). The construction of lessons in effective and less effective classrooms. *Teaching & Teacher Education, 4*(3), 189–213.

Wiederholt, J. L., Hammill, D. D., & Brown, V. L. (1983). *The resource teacher: A guide to effective practices* (2nd ed.). Boston: Allyn and Bacon.

Wolf, M. (1978). Social validation: The case for subjective measurement or How applied behavior analysis is finding its heart. *Journal of Applied Behavioral Analysis, 11*, 203–214.

Ysseldyke, J. E., Thurlow, M. L., Christenson, S. L., & Weiss, J. (1987). Time allocated for instruction of mentally retarded, learning disabled, emotionally disturbed, and nonhandicapped elementary students. *Journal of Special Education, 21*(3), 43–55.

Ysseldyke, J. E., Thurlow, M. L., Mecklenberg, C., & Graden, J. (1984). Opportunity to learn for regular and special education students during reading instruction. *RASE, 5*(1), 29–37.

CEC Mini-Library
Working with Behavioral Disorders

Edited by Lyndal M. Bullock and Robert B. Rutherford, Jr.

A set of nine books developed with the practitioner in mind.

Use this Mini-Library as a reference to help staff understand the problems of specific groups of youngsters with behavioral problems.

- *Teaching Students with Behavioral Disorders: Basic Questions and Answers.* Timothy J. Lewis, Juane Heflin, & Samuel A. DiGangi. No. P337. 1991. 37 pages.

- *Conduct Disorders and Social Maladjustments: Policies, Politics, and Programming.* Frank H. Wood, Christine O. Cheney, Daniel H. Cline, Kristina Sampson, Carl R. Smith, & Eleanor C. Guetzloe. No. P338. 1991. 27 pages.

- *Behaviorally Disordered? Assessment for Identification and Instruction.* Bob Algozzine, Kathy Ruhl, & Roberta Ramsey, No. P339. 1991. 37 pages.

- *Preparing to Integrate Students with Behavioral Disorders.* Robert A. Gable, Virginia K. Laycock, Sharon A. Maroney, & Carl R. Smith. No. P340. 1991. 35 pages

- *Teaching Young Children with Behavioral Disorders.* Mary Kay Zabel. No. P341. 1991. 25 pages.

- *Reducing Undesirable Behaviors.* Edited by Lewis Polsgrove. No. P342. 1991. 33 pages.

- *Social Skills for Students with Autism.* Richard L. Simpson, Brenda Smith Myles, Gary M. Sasso, & Debra M. Kamps. No. P343. 1991. 23 pages.

- *Special Education in Juvenile Corrections.* Peter E. Leone, Robert B. Rutherford, Jr., & C. Michael Nelson. No. P344. 1991. 26 pages.

- *Moving On: Transitions for Youth with Behavioral Disorders.* Michael Bullis & Robert Gaylord-Ross. No. P345. 1991. 52 pages.

Save 10% by ordering the entire library, No. P346, 1991. Call for the most current price information, 703/264-9467.

Send orders to:
The Council for Exceptional Children, Dept. K10350
1920 Association Drive, Reston VA 22091-1589